Making Things

A Book of Days
for the Creative Spirit

Janet Carija Brandt

Martingale®
& C O M P A N Y

Credits

President: Nancy J. Martin
CEO: Daniel J. Martin
Publisher: Jane Hamada
Editorial Director: Mary V. Green
Managing Editor: Tina Cook
Copy Editor: Durby Peterson
Design Director: Stan Green
Cover and Text Designer: Regina Girard
Photographer: Brent Kane

Martingale®
& C O M P A N Y

That
Patchwork
Place®

That Patchwork Place® is an imprint of Martingale & Company®.

Making Things: A Book of Days for the Creative Spirit © 2005 by Janet Carija Brandt

Martingale & Company
20205 144th Avenue NE
Woodinville, WA 98072-8478 USA
www.martingale-pub.com

Printed in China
10 09 08 07 06 05   8 7 6 5 4 3 2 1

Mission Statement
Dedicated to providing
quality products and service
to inspire creativity.

Library of Congress Cataloging-in-Publication Data is available upon request.
ISBN: 1-56477-615-8

Introduction

I've had "makethingitis" all of my life. The things in my case are quilts, rugs, embroideries, and countless other textile objects. Along the way I've also managed to make a marriage, family, and home. Each person has a calling to make something different. The things aren't always craft projects—they can be anything from a space station to tonight's dinner. You can make a lonely person smile or a door hinge stop squeaking.

I love to make things. Along with the observations of a creative lifetime, this book presents some of the final product of this "making things" energy. The photographs feature a new collection of appliquéd, embroidered, and quilted textiles. I have come to realize that what I do, what I am able to do, is a gift, although at various times I have thought of this as a compulsion, mania, hobby, diversion, profession, or great fuel for a bonfire.

The creative life, like any other, has its ups and downs. Enjoy this little book each time you add an important new date in your life or remember an old one. Or enjoy the book just for itself. Sometimes one new thought is all it takes for us to see the daily workings of our lives in a different light.

My views as set forth in this book are based on my personal experience. Enjoy what works for you; leave the rest behind.

Janet Carija Brandt

January

1	New Year's Day
2	
3	
4	
5	
6	
7	

Making Things

In the United States we have grown far removed from the creative process.
Everyone talks about making money, but there are so many other things
to make. The modern person wants to return handmade objects to her life.
Now, making things by hand is a luxury; earlier, it was a necessity.
What was once frugality is now fantasy.

January

8	
9	
10	
11	
12	
13	
14	

Making Wishes

Stores, books, Web sites, and videos give us many ideas for crafts, cooking, decorating, and home improvement. Just as toy catalogs were the wish books of our youth, how-to books filled with instructions and inspirations are our wish books now. Our new wishes are attainable and provide more than just a finished product. They provide satisfaction and pleasure in the hours of planning, making, and use.

January

15	
16	
17	
18	
19	
20	
21	

Making Friends

Keep company with kindred spirits. People who make things have a combination of creativity, generosity, and energy that is contagious. Wander through any craft store, garden show, music festival, or any one of countless weekend events around the country. You will be amazed at the large number of busy people and motivated by the enthusiasm you find.

January

22	
23	
24	
25	
26	
27	
28	

Making Enthusiasm

You know when something interests you. It takes hold of your heart and won't let go. Don't be swayed by the crowd when searching for your personal source of enthusiasm. Be on the lookout for whatever might trigger that inner fire in you. It could show up anywhere at any time, or it might hark back to an interest or activity that you loved as a child.

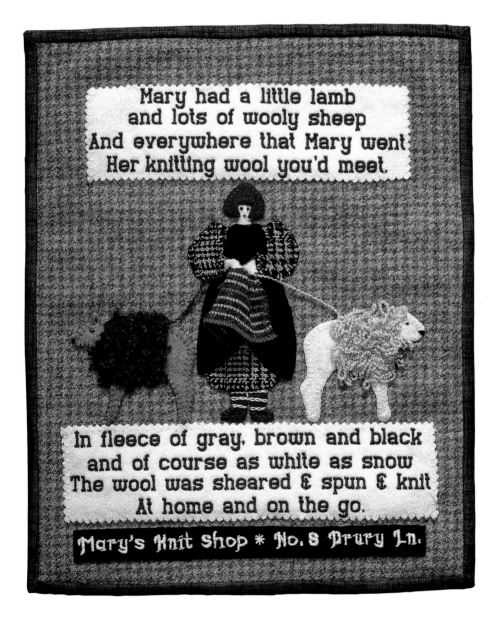

January

29	
30	
31	

Making Our Spirits Happy

One way to feed our souls is through the creative process. Learning about our soul or spirit or inner self is like looking up a gently spiraling stair. There is always something more, something new just around the curve, just out of sight. A ray of light might illuminate one spot while the step beyond waits in darkness. Does the flight end? Continue upward? Is there a door? Is it open? Closed? The only way to find out is to climb the stair.

February

1	
2	Groundhog Day
3	
4	
5	
6	
7	

Making a Start

Making things is personal. It isn't the same as buying a mass-produced item. If you are new to making things, kits and classes are great ways to start a creative adventure. The materials and instructions are handy and the outcome is predictable, but you can personalize it if you want. Self-help books are like kits: they get you started. As you gain skills, you gain confidence, which helps you gain more skills, which gives you more confidence. This is a nice cycle to get into.

February

8	
9	
10	
11	
12	
13	
14	Valentine's Day

Making It Slowly

No thing great is created suddenly, any more than
a bunch of grapes or a fig. If you tell me that you
desire a fig, I answer you that there must be time.
Let it first blossom, then bear fruit, then ripen.

Epictetus

February

| 15 |
| 16 |
| 17 |
| 18 |
| 19 |
| 20 |
| 21 |

Making Potential

I love watching a new home being built. The wood frame
is filled with potential. How will the space be finished,
what purpose will it fill, and most important, how will
people feel within it? We, too, are buildings constantly
under construction. How will we be finished? What
purpose will we fill? How will we feel within ourselves?

February

22

23

24

25

26

27

28/29

Making a Home

Home. It isn't a house or an address. It isn't a certain style of decor.
It is a haven, refuge, and gathering spot. It is making
people feel comfortable, happy, loved, and valued.

March

1

2

3

4

5

6

7

Making It Perfect

A job that's done well can often look so effortless. We don't see the practice, the preparation, and all the background work that went into the final product. It is the sign of a pro—like an athlete, a public speaker, or a performer—to make an action look effortless. But don't be discouraged if your first efforts are not perfect. No one's are. One saying goes, "You do best what you do most." Another says, "The used key shines brightest." And of course everyone has heard "Practice makes perfect," but we all hope to skip the practice part and move right on to perfection!

March

8	
9	
10	
11	
12	
13	
14	

Making Ends Meet

"Making ends meet" is a phrase that's common enough when
balancing your checkbook but just as important when balancing
your creative life. Practice is one form of making ends meet.
The beauty of practice is that the ends are always growing
and therefore meeting with greater ease.

March

15	
16	
17	St. Patrick's Day
18	
19	
20	
21	

Making History

The opposite of war is not peace.
It is making things.

March

22	
23	
24	
25	
26	
27	
28	

Making Progress

At a local doll show an artist showed me both the very first doll
she had made and her most recent doll. She radiated as she spoke
of her work and how much better she felt it had grown.
It showed in her work. It glowed in her eyes!

We each start a new endeavor at our own level. How far we rise
from that point depends entirely on how much time and effort
we are willing to give it. But as soon as we have made our
first effort, we have made a great advance.

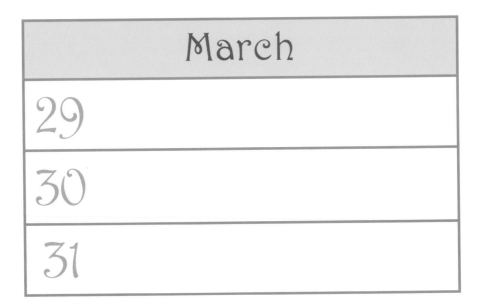

March

29	
30	
31	

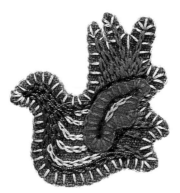

Making Dreams

People smiled, laughed, and doubted when
I first said I wanted to write books.

I smiled and laughed too. I never doubted.

April

1	April Fools' Day
2	
3	
4	
5	
6	
7	

Making Excuses

We are all afraid of not doing IT right. IT can be anything.
I try not to be intimidated by phony rules. The only real mistake
I can make is to not try. The excuses I make for not trying
something new always amaze me. They are usually very weak.
I'm probably not alone. Recognizing the excuse for what it is, is
the first part of fixing the problem. Taking action is the second.

April

8	
9	
10	
11	
12	
13	
14	
15	

Making Commitments

I can make a commitment
or I can make an excuse.
It is my choice.

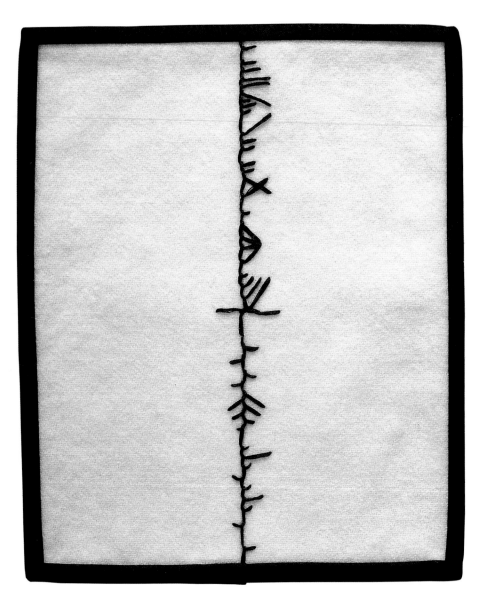

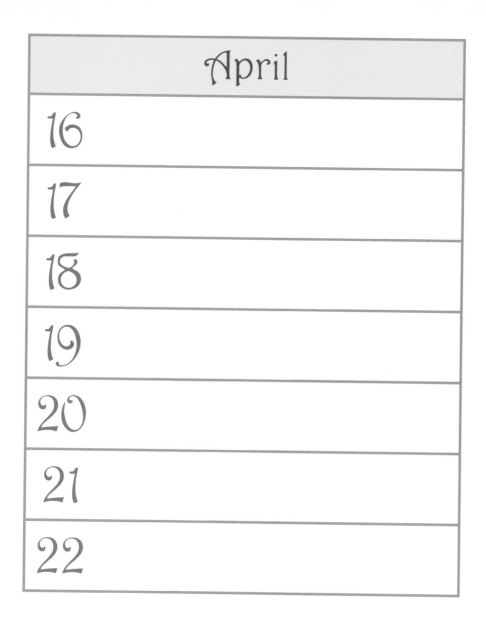

April

16	
17	
18	
19	
20	
21	
22	

Making Adjustments

Here are a few possible variations of one basic embroidery stitch.
By making very small adjustments, I can change
the total look of the stitch. My day can be the same way.
By taking a moment to smile, relax, listen, or hug,
I completely change the moment and, therefore, the day.

April

23	
24	
25	
26	
27	
28	
29	
30	

Making Time

I find the time for things that are important to me. I don't waste time on projects I have outgrown. I don't waste it on battles that ended a long time ago. Think of each minute of each day as a different stitch. What kind of sampler do you plan to stitch today?

May

1

2

3

4

5
Cinco de Mayo

6

7

Making Contentment

One who is content with what he has, and who accepts the fact
that he inevitably will miss out on some things in life, is far better
off than one who has much more, but who worries about all he may
be missing. For we cannot make the best of what we are, if our
hearts are always divided over what we are and what we are not.

Thomas Merton

May

8

9

10

11

12

13

14

15

Making the Best of It

I've always been happy in the world of making things. One of
the beauties of the creative process is this: Just when you think you have
exhausted all your possibilities, a new thought, idea, avenue, process, or
option opens before you, and the creative work begins anew.

May

16	
17	
18	
19	
20	
21	
22	
23	

Making Discoveries

Enquire Within Upon Anything was the title of a
Victorian-era encyclopedia. Make it the goal of your life.

May

24	
25	
26	
27	
28	
29	
30	
31	

Making Words

Sometimes I just want to make lots of words on a page
instead of drawings or designs. I can't always choose
what I am going to make. The creative voice inside me
finds the best way to make itself known, if I just listen.

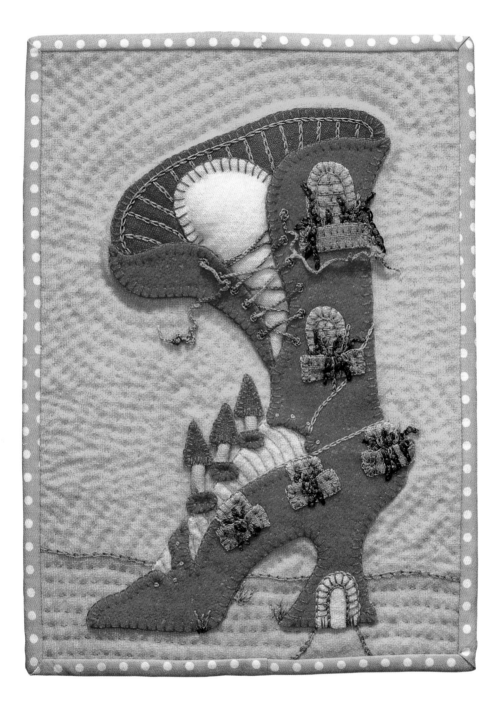

June

1	
2	
3	
4	
5	
6	
7	

Making Plans

What would a scrapbook of your creative life look like?
What do you want it to look like?

June

8

9

10

11

12

13

14
Flag Day

Making Inspiration

What whets your creative appetite? Music, poetry, nature,
a museum, or colored paper and a jar of paste? The junkyard,
a craft store, or a gourmet shop? Books, TV, or magazines? An
unsolved math problem, a devastating disease, or an engineering
dilemma? Friends, neighbors, or family? Poverty, crime, or illiteracy?
All of the above? None of the above? Find it. Encourage it.

June

15

16

17

18

19

20

21

Making a Contribution

I know I am not the only person who feels compelled
to make things. Church bazaars, community events, and
school fundraisers are just a few of the places filled with
the bounty of creativity. The spirit behind the product
and the pride of the accomplishment are inspiring.

June

22	
23	
24	
25	
26	
27	
28	

Making Room for Downtime

When I don't want to make things, I don't. I might go for a walk,
clean a closet, read a book, count stars, or listen to the grass grow,
but I don't think of this time as unproductive. Downtime is very useful.
It allows me to step away from an activity and later return with a new
perspective. Don't fight the instinct to step back and regroup.

June

29	
30	

Making a Plea

There are only two verses of anything that I have been able
to commit to memory in my life. One is a poem about
a purple cow, and the other is this prayer:

Lord, make me an instrument of Your peace. Where there is
hatred let me sow love; where there is injury, pardon; where there
is doubt, faith; where there is despair, hope; where there is
darkness, light; and where there is sadness, joy.

O divine Master, grant that I may not so much seek to be
consoled as to console; to be understood as to understand;
to be loved as to love. For it is in giving that we receive;
it is in pardoning that we are pardoned; and it is
in dying that we are born to eternal life.

St. Francis of Assisi

July

1   Canada Day

2

3

4   Independence Day

5

6

7

8

Making Do
Use it up, wear it out;
Make it do, or do without.
New England maxim

July

9	
10	
11	
12	
13	
14	
15	
16	

Making Music

I have no musical talent, so when I listen to music that I love,
it reminds me to be thankful for and focus on those things
that I can do. It also reminds me to enjoy the creative
labors of others with talents I don't have.

July

17

18

19

20

21

22

23

24

Making Love
God is love. Love is the only answer.

July

25	
26	
27	
28	
29	
30	
31	

Making Peace

The fruit of silence is prayer,
the fruit of prayer is faith,
the fruit of faith is love,
the fruit of love is service,
and the fruit of service is peace.
Mother Teresa

August

1

2

3

4

5

6

7

Making Prayer
Make it a habit to talk to God.
Check in a couple times a day to thank,
praise, question, or just chat.

August

8

9

10

11

12

13

14

Making the World a Better Place

Don't add to the anger of the world.
There is too much already. Everyone can help make
the world a better place in her or his own way.

August

15	
16	
17	
18	
19	
20	
21	

Making a Balanced Life

On Sunday nights my husband and I go to our local Mexican restaurant
for dinner. I always order the #2 combo. I like it, I look forward to it,
and there are no surprises. In my work I rarely make the same thing twice.
I can't wait to move on to the next challenge, the next unknown.
It may sound silly, but this is one small way of balancing my life.

August

22	
23	
24	
25	
26	
27	
28	

Making Much of Little

I spent the afternoon at an American Indian Museum.
I was amazed anew by the beautiful objects that have
been created from the most basic of materials. It is a great
reminder that it isn't about how much money you spend
on materials or equipment; it's about taking the
time to learn, to practice, and to create.

August

29	
30	
31	

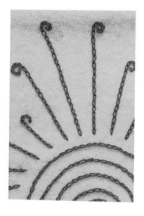

Making Priorities

I learned a long time ago that the project I most want to work on is not usually the one that needs to be worked on. I call it the greener-grass syndrome. I want a different project, goal, talent, job, or friend—anything instead of savoring what I have in my hands.

HORNER'S ORCHARD
Plums, Peaches, Apples & Pears
PICK YOUR OWN
DAILY 8 AM TO 8 PM

September

1	
2	
3	
4	
5	
6	
7	

Making a Smile

Watch the reaction to a smile, whether it's a smile you give
or one you receive. The creative spirit is only as rich as what
we invest in it. A smile costs nothing but rewards you many
times over. Put a smile on your creative spirit. It will leap for joy.

September

8	
9	
10	
11	
12	
13	
14	

Making Creative Children

I think creativity is one of the most powerful human traits we possess.
When we deprive children of arts programs, we aren't taking away busywork.
We are taking away a chance to learn problem-solving skills. Life is nothing
but full-time problem solving, so why not learn to do it creatively?

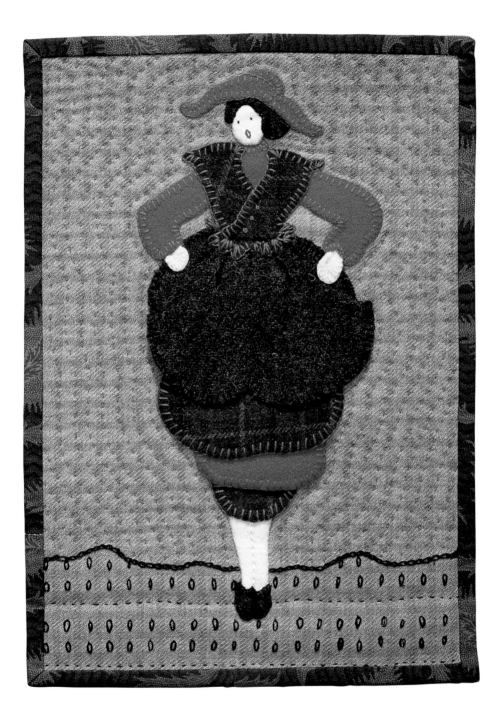

September

15	
16	
17	
18	
19	
20	
21	
22	

Making Nourishment

Every day I get to choose how to feed myself. I know that a steady diet of junk food is bad for my body, so it makes sense not to feed my mind and soul junk either. What will I listen to, read, watch, or participate in? I can grow in a positive direction every day.

September

23	
24	
25	
26	
27	
28	
29	
30	

Making Kindness

No act of kindness, no matter how small, is ever wasted.

Aesop

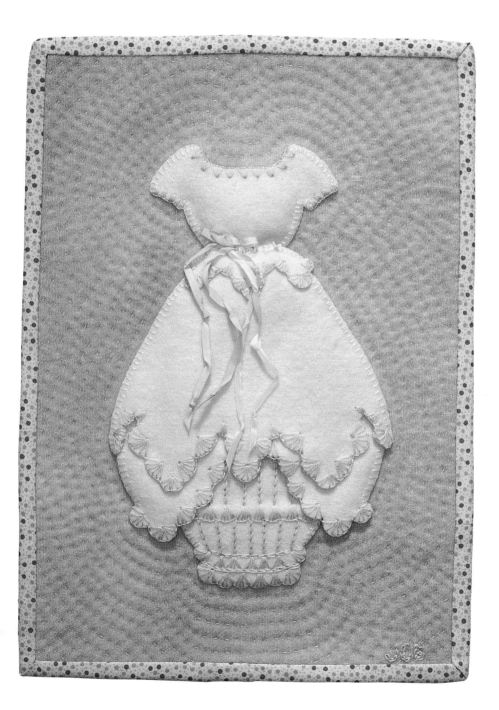

October

1	
2	
3	
4	
5	
6	
7	

Making Journals

The creative voice inside me is a pack rat. Just as I have a
hard time parting with an object that I might find a use for later,
so I also hoard ideas and thoughts. I fill notebooks and
journals. They're giant scrapbooks of the brain.

October

8	
9	
10	
11	
12	
13	
14	

Making Beginnings

People are always blaming their circumstances for what they are.
I don't believe in circumstances. The people who get on in this world
are the people who get up and look for the circumstances they want,
and, if they can't find them, make them.

George Bernard Shaw

October

15

16

17

18

19

20

21

Making Enough

As the saying goes, "Enough is as good as a feast."
It's easy to think of those words in terms of food, but
they could apply to anything. Do we really know how much
is enough? Or are we ever content with enough when we
have so much more than what we need in the first place?

October

22	
23	
24	
25	
26	
27	
28	

Making Creativity

Creativity is using the resources you best understand to
make something positive happen. This isn't just about the arts.
It's about business, medicine, leadership, housekeeping,
world politics, or a Sunday potluck dinner.

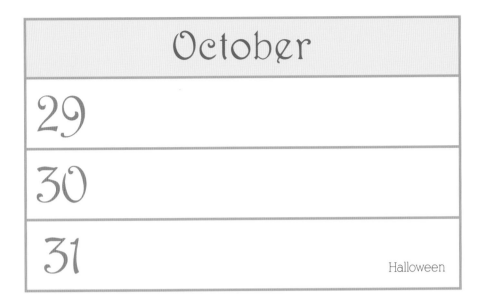

October

29	
30	
31	Halloween

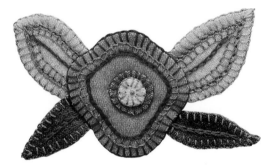

Making It Anyway

If you sing a song, plant a garden, or paint a picture, and
you are the only one to hear the song, smell the flowers,
or see the painting, these are efforts worth making.

November

1	
2	
3	
4	
5	
6	
7	

Making Happy Thoughts

The world is so full of a number of things,
I'm sure we should all be as happy as kings.
Robert Louis Stevenson

November

8

9

10

11

Veterans Day

12

13

14

15

Making Requests

Ask and you shall receive.
Sometimes it is as simple as that.

November

16	
17	
18	
19	
20	
21	
22	
23	

Making Squeaks

The squeaky wheel gets the grease.
Be the squeaky wheel when it comes to your own well-being
and the well-being of your family and community.

November

24	
25	
26	
27	
28	
29	
30	

Making Waves

Sometimes squeaks aren't loud enough to foster the changes that are needed. That's when you need to make waves. Are there dangerous activities in your neighborhood? Is pollution choking your air and water? Are there people in your community who are hungry and homeless? Are children being denied the education they need? These issues are always calling for creative people to step up, make waves, and make a difference.

December

1	
2	
3	
4	
5	
6	
7	

Making the Moment Count

You've got to accentuate the positive
Eliminate the negative
And latch on to the affirmative
Don't mess with Mister In-Between
Lyrics by Johnny Mercer

December

8	
9	
10	
11	
12	
13	
14	

Making Merry

There is nothing better for a man than that he should
eat and drink, and find enjoyment in his toil.

Ecclesiastes 2:24

December

15	
16	
17	
18	
19	
20	
21	

Making Observations

The lacy web of bare branches against the gray sky looks cold and forlorn. But then I pick out two furry dots, two squirrels with their tails wrapped over them in the cold wind, noisily chattering to one another. On another branch a woodpecker is hard at work. And I watch birds gather and feast on this year's bounty of ornamental pears. It is cold but not forlorn out there.

December

22	
23	
24	
25	Christmas Day
26	First Day of Kwanzaa
27	
28	

Making an Effort

I'm watching the snow falling on a pond. Some flakes hardly make an impression on the water; others send tiny ripples skimming across the surface. On the ground the snow is starting to stick. It is accumulating in the pond as well, but its accumulation there is invisible. Like the snow, my efforts sometimes amount to something tangible and at other times seem to make no difference. But the ripples prove that snow is falling on the pond. And my efforts, whether their results are visible or not, are making their own ripples in my history. If it snows long enough, the pond will be snow-covered too.

December

29	
30	
31	New Year's Eve

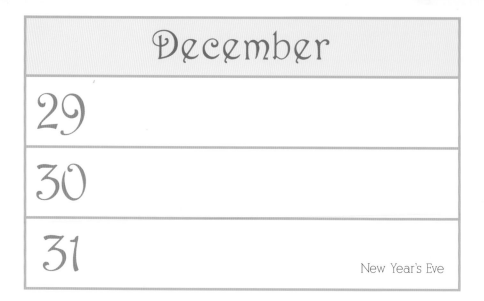

Making It Easy

You've been a creative person waiting to blossom all along.
Now:
Recognize the many creative aspects of your life,
Set your goals,
Unleash your creative spirit—MAKE THINGS!

About the Author

Janet Carija Brandt lives in Indianapolis, Indiana, with her husband. She has worked with textiles in one way or another most of her life. She continues to enjoy all of the wonderful traditional skills of appliqué, embroidery, and rug hooking, while also embracing the twenty-first century and the wonders of digitized embroidery and embroidery machines. Janet also works as a designer for Husqvarna Viking, expanding the conventions of two-dimensional machine embroidery into three-dimensional dolls and miniature theaters. Most of all, Janet hopes you will enjoy making things now and for the rest of your long creative life.